Blitzed by a BLIZZARD!

Disaster SURVIVORS

by Joyce Markovics

Consultants:

Daphne Thompson, Meteorologist
Educational Outreach Coordinator
Cooperative Institute for Mesoscale Meteorological Studies
National Weather Center

Keith C. Heidorn, Ph.D.
CMOS Accredited Consulting Meteorologist (retired)
Publisher and Editor of *The Weather Doctor* Web site

BEARPORT
PUBLISHING

New York, New York

Credits

Cover, © Peter Gudella/Shutterstock and © Serghei Starus/Shutterstock; Back Cover and Title Page, © Quanthem/Shutterstock; TOC, © Marketa Ebert/iStockphoto; 4–5, © Bill Stevenson/Purestock/SuperStock; 6, Courtesy of Randy Kraxberger; 7, © Sandy Macys/Alamy; 8, © Steve Ringman/Seattle Times/MCT/Landov; 9, © Gordon Wiltsie/NGS Images; 10, © moodboard/SuperStock; 11, © Ashley Cooper/Corbis; 12L, © The Granger Collection, New York; 12R, © The Granger Collection, New York; 13, © The Granger Collection, New York; 15T, © Bettmann/Corbis; 15B, © Wallace G. Levison/Time Life Pictures/Getty Images; 17, © Jim Zuckerman/Corbis; 18L, © Erik Simonsen/Photographer's Choice/Getty Images; 18R, © AP Images/Ric Feld; 19, © Dainis Derics/Shutterstock; 20, © Everett Collection; 21T, © Acey Harper/Time Life Pictures/Getty Images; 21B, © Sandra Mu/Getty Images; 22, © Gary C. Caskey/UPI Photo/Landov; 23T, © AP Images/Will Powers; 23B, © Gary C. Caskey/UPI Photo/Landov; 24–25, © Xinhua/Landov; 26, Courtesy of the National Park Service; 27, © AP Images/Justine Sutcliffe; 28, © AP Images/Walter Stein; 29, © JJ pixs/Shutterstock.

Publisher: Kenn Goin
Editorial Director: Adam Siegel
Creative Director: Spencer Brinker
Design: Dawn Beard Creative
Photo Researcher: Amy Dunleavy

Library of Congress Cataloging-in-Publication Data

Markovics, Joyce L.
  Blitzed by a blizzard! / by Joyce Markovics ; consultant, Daphne Thompson.
      p. cm. — (Disaster survivors)
  Includes bibliographical references and index.
  ISBN-13: 978-1-936087-54-9 (lib. bdg.)
  ISBN-10: 1-936087-54-5 (lib. bdg.)
  1. Blizzards—Juvenile literature. 2. Emergency management—Juvenile literature. I. Title.
  QC926.37.M37 2010
  551.55'5—dc22
                              2009036960

For more information, write to Bearport Publishing Company, Inc., 101 Fifth Avenue, Suite 6R, New York, New York 10003. Printed in the United States of America in North Mankato, Minnesota.

122009
090309CGE

10 9 8 7 6 5 4 3 2 1

Contents

Whiteout!

The sky was clear when skier Randy Kraxberger left the visitor center at Olympic National Park in Washington State. It was December 29, 2007, and Randy was looking forward to skiing alone near Hurricane Hill. After several hours of skiing, the sky began filling with snow. "The **tracks** got covered up fairly fast," Randy said. The trail soon disappeared under a blanket of white.

With the snow came fierce winds. **Ice crystals** blasted Randy's face. The sky grew dark as the swirling snow shut out the sun's light. Randy was trapped in a **whiteout**. He couldn't see through the heavy snow, and he had no idea where he was.

During a whiteout, heavy blowing snow makes it impossible to see anything. As a result, people caught in whiteouts often become lost, even if they are very close to safety.

A Snowy Blast

Randy found himself lost in a **blizzard**—the most extreme kind of winter storm. A blizzard combines heavy snow with winds that blow 35 miles per hour (56 kph) or more. During a blizzard, **visibility** is very poor. The blowing snow stops people from seeing more than a quarter mile (.4 km) in front of them for at least three hours.

Randy took this photo of himself during the blizzard.

Luckily, Randy had a backpack and cell phone with him. He immediately called his wife Lisa, who put him in touch with park rangers. The rangers set out on skis to find Randy. However, wind gusts of 45 miles per hour (72 kph) and the possibility of **avalanches** forced some of them to turn back. It would soon be dark. With no help in sight, Randy had to do something quickly or risk freezing to death.

In the winter, park rangers often use skis to reach people who are trapped in the snow.

Surviving the Night

It was getting colder as the sun set. Randy hiked to a cluster of pine trees to find shelter. There, he dug a cave out of snow and crawled inside. He hoped that the snow cave would protect him from the freezing winds.

This woman chips away at icy snow to make a cave.

A snow cave keeps people warm in a way that is similar to an **igloo**. The inside of the cave stays warmer than the outside air because the cave's snowy walls trap air, keeping heat from escaping.

Once inside, Randy searched his backpack. "I saw that I had some **chemical hand warmers**," Randy recalls, "so I knew that would be good for later." To keep his body from getting too cold, Randy exercised every few hours. About 15 inches (38 cm) of snow fell during the night, but Randy was still able to stay fairly warm inside his snow cave.

Travelers wait inside their snow cave for a storm to end.

X Marks the Spot

In the morning, Randy awoke to find snow piled on his nose and his beard frozen. He called the park rangers to tell them where he was located. They sent a helicopter and a team on foot. Using his skis and tree branches, Randy made a large X in the snow. There he waited for the helicopter, but it never came. Would the rescuers ever reach him?

Bad weather kept the helicopter from rescuing Randy.

People stranded in the wilderness are often too small to be seen by a helicopter or plane. Rescuers are more likely to spot them if they create a large marker, such as an X, on the ground.

Suddenly, Randy heard something. "I was standing there on the X, and I could hear voices," Randy remembers. He quickly blew the whistle he had brought to get their attention. To his relief, he saw people coming over a hill toward him. At last, Randy would be saved!

Rescue workers often bring stretchers with them in case the people they find can't walk.

"The Schoolchildren's Blizzard"

Randy was lucky to have survived a blizzard. Others have not been so fortunate. One of the worst blizzards in U.S. history took place in the northern Great Plains in 1888. At that time, people didn't have the **technology** to **forecast** storms as well as they do today. They also couldn't send out warnings quickly, since television and radio hadn't been invented yet. As a result, the blizzard took everyone by surprise.

The blizzard hit Nebraska and today's South Dakota very hard. These drawings show rescue workers searching for survivors.

The morning of January 12, 1888, was a warm winter's day. In fact, it was so warm that children walked to school without coats or gloves. However, the weather changed quickly. Within a few hours, a powerful blizzard struck. As students walked home in the blinding snow, many lost their way. Others tumbled into **snowdrifts**. That night, the temperature fell as much as 50 degrees Fahrenheit (28 degrees Celsius)! By the next day, the bodies of those trapped by the storm lay frozen on the ground.

A teacher and her student walking through the blizzard

Between 250 and 500 people died in the 1888 blizzard. About 100 of them were children. For this reason, the storm became known as "The Schoolchildren's Blizzard."

Another Deadly Storm

Later that year, in March 1888, another killer storm hit the United States. This time it struck the East Coast. The blizzard dropped up to four feet (1.2 m) of snow in some areas. Wind gusts of up to 80 miles per hour (129 kph) knocked over **power lines** and created huge snowdrifts. One New Yorker described "drifts as high as the second stories" of buildings.

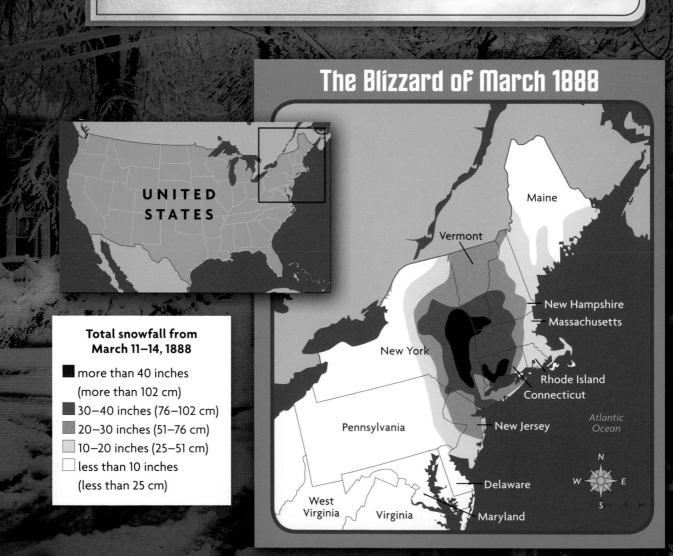

The Blizzard of March 1888

UNITED STATES

Maine

Vermont

New Hampshire

Massachusetts

New York

Rhode Island

Connecticut

Atlantic Ocean

Pennsylvania

New Jersey

Delaware

West Virginia

Virginia

Maryland

Total snowfall from March 11–14, 1888

- more than 40 inches (more than 102 cm)
- 30–40 inches (76–102 cm)
- 20–30 inches (51–76 cm)
- 10–20 inches (25–51 cm)
- less than 10 inches (less than 25 cm)

N
W E
S

The storm **paralyzed** New York City. Businesses shut down, the Brooklyn Bridge closed, and trains and streetcars crawled to a stop. Thousands of workers were stranded across the city, unable to get home. When the blizzard was over, it had caused about $25 million in damage.

The Blizzard of 1888 knocked over these power lines.

About 400 people were killed during the 1888 blizzard. Most died when they got lost in the snow or stuck in snowdrifts.

The 1888 blizzard led to the construction of subways and underground power lines in New York City. They were built because it is very hard for blizzards to damage these underground structures.

Recipe for Disaster

What causes snowstorms and blizzards? They both begin with storm clouds. These clouds form when warm and cold **air masses** in the sky crash into each other. The heavier cold air forces the lighter warm air to rise above it. The warm air cools as it rises, causing **water vapor** in the air to turn into water droplets that form clouds.

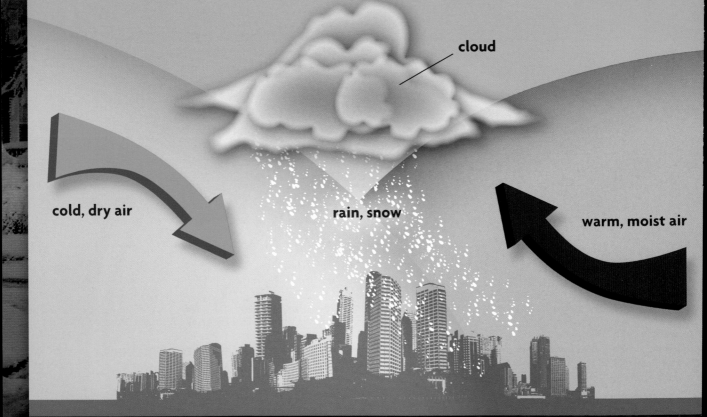

How Storm Clouds Form

cloud

cold, dry air

rain, snow

warm, moist air

In order for the droplets to freeze and turn to snow, the air temperature within the clouds and near the ground must be less than 32°F (0°C). If the air is too warm, the moisture that falls will be rain, not snow.

Snowflakes are made from crystals of ice. The ice crystals form around tiny pieces of dust that are in the clouds. A single snowflake may contain up to 200 ice crystals.

Predicting Blizzards

Thanks to new technology, scientists have become better at predicting winter storms. **Meteorologists** use special tools to forecast the weather. For example, **satellites** measure air temperature and take pictures of the clouds and storms above Earth. **Radar** equipment on the ground and aboard special planes also gathers information about clouds and the sizes of snowflakes and raindrops.

Some weather satellites orbit Earth 14 times each day.

Meteorologists analyzing weather data

Meteorologists study this information for signs of an oncoming winter storm. Once meteorologists know for certain that a storm is on its way, they use radio or television to warn people about the danger.

People feel colder on a windy day because the wind causes the body to lose heat.

Meteorologists often describe the temperature during a blizzard using the windchill factor. This number shows how cold people feel as a result of the wind. The stronger the wind blows, the colder people feel—even if the air temperature is the same.

Blizzard Travel

Despite advances in forecasting, blizzards are still dangerous, especially for travelers. During a blizzard, roads can become icy and blocked by snow.

In December 1992, the Stolpa family became stranded on a road while driving in a Nevada blizzard. Stuck in the middle of nowhere, James Stolpa left his wife and five-month-old son behind to find help. "If I had stayed there, then we all would have died," he said.

This scene is from the 1994 movie *Snowbound*, which was based on the Stolpas' story.

James trudged through the snow, hoping someone would find him. Finally, after walking nearly 50 miles (80 km), he was spotted by a passing driver who brought him to safety. James then called rescuers, who were able to find his family. Both James and his wife Jennifer lost all their toes to **frostbite**, but the family survived.

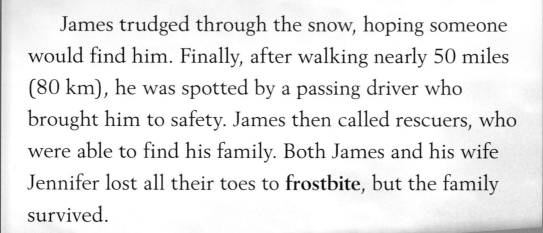

James, Jennifer, and their son Clayton after they were rescued

Frostbitten fingers

Frostbite occurs when body parts such as fingers or toes freeze solid. In severe cases, blood cannot reach the frozen area, and it turns black and dies.

A Big White Headache

Not all blizzards end in disaster. Almost all, however, cause major **inconveniences**. On December 20, 2006, a blizzard in Colorado dumped close to 30 inches (76 cm) of snow in the Denver area. "It was an adventure like I've never had before," said Mary Zamora, who was stuck on a bus for more than three hours.

People in Denver braved the 2006 storm to buy groceries and supplies.

The Denver blizzard also brought the city's airport to a standstill. More than 2,500 flights were canceled. Thousands of travelers were stranded. In addition, highways, post offices, and shops all closed down. Most workers headed home. Receptionist Christen Amdahl said, "It's like the city is shutting down . . . It's fun, but it's kind of a hassle."

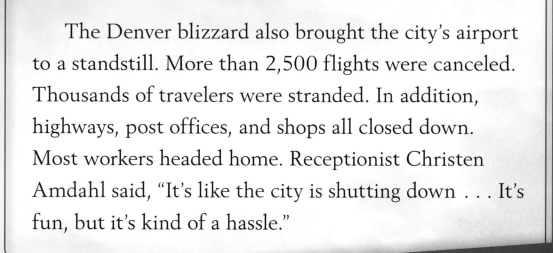

During the Denver blizzard, around 5,000 people were left stranded at the Denver International Airport.

There's a lot of cleaning up to do after a blizzard.

The Other Side of the World

People around the world—not just in the United States—have to battle blizzards. In mid-January 2008, as millions of people in China traveled home for the Chinese New Year holiday, a giant storm hit.

For almost two weeks, blizzards and ice storms raged across southern China. Roads were shut down and trains canceled, leading to a **transportation** nightmare. Hundreds of thousands of Chinese people were left stranded at train stations. Wang Jigen, a worker forced to wait in the slushy mess, said, "I have no idea where I'll sleep tonight or how I'll ever get home."

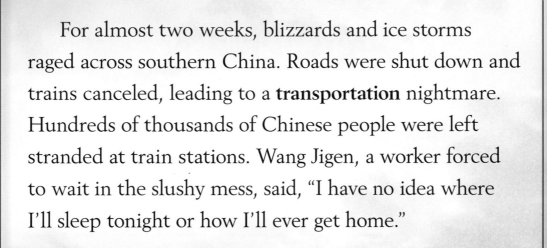

Cold, tired passengers in China wait to get into the railway station.

In 1972, a weeklong blizzard hit Iran. It dumped up to 26 feet (8 m) of snow in some areas, killing around 4,000 people.

To Ski Another Day

When rescuers reached Randy Kraxberger, he was exhausted but thankful to be alive. Despite being trapped in a blizzard overnight, Randy felt well enough to ski back to the visitor center with the park rangers.

The park rangers who rescued Randy received an award for their courage.

Following his rescue, Randy thought about what he could have done differently. He wished he had brought a flashlight, a blanket, and more food and clothing. Also, Randy regretted not paying attention to a storm warning he had heard at the visitor center the previous day. "I wish I had taken that more seriously," he said. A blizzard is something *everyone* should take seriously.

The 1993 blizzard didn't stop these New Yorkers from getting to their jobs.

The largest blizzard in the United States in recent years hit the Northeast in 1993 and caused more than 300 deaths. The storm dropped almost four feet (1.2 m) of snow in some areas.

Famous Blizzards

The United States has a long history of dangerous blizzards. Here are a few that have resulted in widespread destruction and many deaths.

The Big Blow, 1913

- The Big Blow hit the Great Lakes area in mid-November 1913.
- Winds reached an incredible 90 miles per hour (145 kph). That's much faster than cars are allowed to travel on a highway.
- The blizzard killed about 250 people. Most of them were aboard ships.

The Knickerbocker Storm, 1922

- As much as three feet (.9 m) of snow fell in Maryland, Virginia, and Pennsylvania in January 1922. In total, the blizzard affected 22,400 square miles (58,016 sq km).
- The storm was named after the Knickerbocker Theater in Washington, D.C. The theater collapsed as a result of the snow and wind, killing 98 people.

The Great Appalachian Storm, 1950

- Blizzard conditions ripped through the eastern United States at the end of November 1950.
- As many as 300 people lost their lives in the freezing temperatures. In Kentucky, the temperature dropped to a bone-chilling −2°F (−19°C).

Cars were buried in snow during the Great Appalachian Storm.

Blizzard Safety

Here are some blizzard safety tips from the National Weather Service:

✔ The best way to stay safe in a blizzard is to avoid getting stuck outside in the first place! So always check weather reports. Here are some different types of winter storm warnings: A *winter storm watch* means that severe winter weather is possible in the next day or two. A *winter storm warning* indicates that severe winter weather will soon begin or has already begun. A *blizzard warning* means that blizzard conditions have developed, and people should stay indoors.

✔ If you are traveling by car, make sure it has snow tires or tire chains and the gas tank is full.

✔ Carry a winter storm survival kit in your car that includes extra clothing, blankets, a flashlight, a first-aid kit, food and water, matches, a shovel, a compass, and road maps.

✔ Finding shelter is crucial if you are caught outside during a blizzard. Learn how to build a snow cave for protection. Exercise to stay warm. Do not eat snow, which will make you colder. Melt it first.

✔ Protect yourself by dressing warmly. Wear many layers of clothing, including a hat and gloves or mittens. Be sure your winter jacket is waterproof and has a hood. In extreme cold, cover your mouth with a scarf to protect your lungs from cold air.

Glossary

air masses (AIR MASS-iz) bodies of air that cover huge areas

avalanches (AV-uh-*lanch*-iz) masses of snow, sometimes containing ice or rocks, that quickly move or slide down mountainsides

blizzard (BLIZ-urd) snow combined with high winds and low visibility

chemical hand warmers (KEM-uh-kuhl HAND WORM-urz) small handheld packets that produce heat

forecast (FOR-kast) to predict the weather

frostbite (FRAWST-*bite*) damage to part of the body due to extreme cold

ice crystals (EYESS KRISS-tuhlz) tiny bits of frozen water

igloo (IG-loo) a domed house made out of hard snow or ice

inconveniences (*in*-kuhn-VEEN-yuhn-suhz) things that cause difficulties or make something harder to do

meteorologists (*mee*-tee-ur-OL-oh-jists) scientists who study and forecast the weather

paralyzed (PA-ruh-lyezd) made something unable to move or function

power lines (POU-ur LYENZ) wires that carry electricity

radar (RAY-dar) a tool that can find the location of an object by sending out radio waves, which hit the object and bounce back to form an image on a computer screen

satellites (SAT-uh-*lyets*) spacecraft that orbit Earth and send information back to scientists

snowdrifts (SNOH-drifts) walls or piles of snow

technology (tek-NOL-uh-jee) the use of science to do practical things

tracks (TRAKS) the marks left behind by something

transportation (*transs*-pur-TAY-shuhn) a system for moving people or goods around

visibility (*viz*-uh-BILL-uh-tee) the distance that an object can be clearly seen

water vapor (WAW-tur VAY-pur) water in the form of a gas

whiteout (WITE-out) a weather condition in which blowing snow makes it impossible to see far

Bibliography

Burt, Christopher C. *Extreme Weather: A Guide and Record Book.* New York: W. W. Norton (2007).

Dickerson, Paige. "Lost Skier Found Atop Hurricane Hill." *Peninsula Daily News* (December 31, 2007).

Laskin, David. *The Children's Blizzard.* New York: HarperCollins (2004).

www.nesec.org/hazards/winter_storms.cfm

www.nws.noaa.gov/om/brochures/wntrstm.htm

Read More

Ball, Jacqueline A. *Blizzard! The 1888 Whiteout (X-treme Disasters That Changed America).* New York: Bearport Publishing (2005).

Murphy, Jim. *Blizzard!* New York: Scholastic Press (2000).

Swails, Terry. *Superstorms: Extreme Weather in the Heart of the Heartland.* Helena, MT: Farcountry Press (2005).

Woods, Michael and Mary B. *Blizzards (Disasters Up Close).* Minneapolis, MN: Lerner Publications (2008).

Learn More Online

To learn more about blizzards, visit
www.bearportpublishing.com/DisasterSurvivors

Index

About the Author

Joyce Markovics is an editor, writer, and orchid collector. When it snows, Joyce enjoys staying indoors with her husband, Adam, and reading books about treacherous winter storms.